Caitlin Kendall's beautiful collection, *Nothing is Yours*, is a poetic chronicle full of wisdom and tenderness which charts three stages of womanhood, with all their familiar intricacies, in new and unexpected ways. There is something to be found for us all in its pages. Kendall has a talent for enchanting the ordinary everyday — the favourite childhood sandwich, the shampoo bottle in the bathroom, the bookshelf in the living room — with a keen observation and generosity that touches all of her work with the spirit of fairytale.

She is an enchantress. These poems are her spells.

Amelia Loulli, Poet

Nothing is Yours

Caitlin Kendall

First published in Great Britain by Bent Key Publishing, 2023
Copyright © Caitlin Kendall, 2023
The moral right of the author has been asserted.

All rights reserved. No part of this book may be reproduced in any form or by any electronic or mechanical means, including information storage and retrieval systems, without permission in writing from the publisher, except by reviewers, who may quote brief passages in a review.

ISBN: 978-1-915320-25-4

Bent Key Publishing
Office 2, Unit 5 Palatine Industrial Estate
Causeway Avenue
Warrington WA4 6QQ
bentkeypublishing.co.uk

Edited by Rebecca Kenny @ Bent Key
Cover art © Samantha Sanderson-Marshall @ SMASH Design and Illustration
smashdesigns.co.uk

Printed in the UK by Mixam UK Ltd.

For Rosie and Jonah, thank you for being the most inspirational thing I have ever created.

For Candy, thank you for loving me through it.

And for anyone caught up in the whirlwind of parenting and battling their own demons: may you find some solace in these pages. You are not alone.

Contents

i. Maiden — 11
    Dewsmoor, 1987 — 13
    Grandma's Kitchen, 1991 — 14
    The Best Sandwich, 1992 — 15
    Summer, 1990 — 16
    Urban Spaceman, 1998 — 17
    Sugar Rush, 2001 — 18

ii. Mother — 19
    Found on a Beach, 2013 — 21
    Things I Learned as a Young Mum, 2003 — 22
    Units of Attention, 2017 — 24
    Shampoo, 2004 — 25
    Ode to a Bookshelf, 2005 — 26
    I Bear Stars on My Hip for You, 2006 — 27
    My Body, 2019 — 28
    That Girl, 2020 — 29

iii. Crone — 31
    Wintering, 2021 — 33
    Ripples, 2021 — 34
    Things I'll Never Do With You Again, 2021 — 35
    Missing a Step on the Stairs, 2016 — 37
    Death is a Woman, 2021 — 38
    By the river at dawn, she digs, 2021 — 39
    Mind the (Sycamore) Gap, c.1700 — 41

Acknowledgements / About the Author — 43
About Bent Key — 43

Nothing is Yours

i.
Maiden

Dewsmoor, 1987

Naked. Standing at the kitchen door, I slip muddy feet into red wellingtons. Each fingernail has its own earthen crescent. In the wellingtons and an upturned bucket hat, I climb the ladder to my treehouse. In the empty wooden doorway, I turn, looking down to the dizzying green carpet. My treehouse has two wooden bunk beds, two chairs around the circular table, it even has red and blue checked curtains at the window. I hear my mother calling me for tea. I descend backwards down the ladder, arriving at the ground arse first. Shaking. When I remove my wellingtons at the kitchen door, red blood pours from my knees.

Grandma's Kitchen, 1991

My favourite job in Grandma's kitchen
was putting away the tea towels.
She had these puckered rubber mouths
stuck to the side of her cupboard.
I used to feed a corner to each one,
pressing my finger tentatively into the cavity,
afraid it might swallow me too,
leaving the towel trailing
like a limp rabbit in the mouth of a fox.
My hands still damp from the dishes
My cheeks sticky with peaches and cream.

The Best Sandwich, 1992

I carried you with me
safe and snug in brown paper
as I trekked and I trudged
following the course set
by those ancient stones.

I carried you with me
buried deep in my pack
as the rain lashed down
soaking the scarf
tied in a knot at my chin.

I carried you with me
with my flask filled with tea
and my map
as I walked the footfalls of those
gone before.

I carried you with me
past the Sycamore Gap
as I hiked with my mother and sisters
Steel Rigg to Housesteads
and back.

I carried you with me
as I sought shelter upon the wall
set down the weight of my pack
and I unwrapped your brown paper
put aside my map and my tea

I ate you; you were so delicious
I carry your memory with me.

Summer, 1990

That was the summer you turned seven and the tar bubbled up from the roads. Your dad showed you how to fry an egg on the bonnet of your brown Volvo estate car.

The winter before, you had stood, barefoot, on the floorboards of your living room and watched the Berlin Wall come down on your 12" TV screen.

It was the summer that the air crackled, so hot your mum brought cold flannels when she came to pick you up from school and talked to you about Greenhouse gases and the Ozone Layer.

That was the summer Mum bought you an ice-cream in the park every day after school; 99s from Mr Curley-top, a white whirl resting on its wafer cone, dripping in monkey's blood with its chocolate flake like a unicorn horn.

It was the summer that Maggie Thatcher resigned and your mum bought you TWO ice-creams after school. You were sticky and happy, your hand speckled with the flaked metallic paint of the playground, the small gravel stones of the springy tarmac between your fingers.

That was the summer you went to a party and waved a paper South Africa flag and your parents told you that a man named Nelson Mandela was finally free. You stood in the darkened community centre and watched the wrinkled images from half the world away on the projector screen as the whole world unfurled before you.

Urban Spaceman, 1998

You're the urban spaceman
Bonzo Dogs and your lips
On my lips. The cool metallic
Taste of your tongue bar
Timid trembling fingers fluttering at my ribs
You've got speed
Spooned in your single bed
Unfolding, your hand
On my breast
You've got everything I need
Fourteen and the first flush
Of lust. Our bildungsroman
                       romance

Sugar Rush, 2001

Today you wore dresses over flares
Ragged ends worn away at the back
Where your trainers had stepped on them
Under your sky-blue ski jacket, your borrowed dress
Was pale and sparkly
                                          It glowed under UV light.
                             Everything was blue in the Bassment.
Today Andy C's pounding bass brought a smile to your face.
     Made you dance
Today, you felt everything
        Dopamine-induced gunpowder love.
it was sugar dusted.
Electric-charged.
                         A force of nature.
You thought it was going to be forever.

ii.
Mother

Found on a Beach, 2013

We rode two buses
and a boat
with its car-tyre buffers
The driftwood pier
We clambered ashore

We searched for shells
lay in the dunes
and watched the clouds
Their shifting shapes
as they sailed by

Our bodies ebbing and flowing
together and apart
as we bathed
We walked in the breakers
as the sun set
kicked their foam heads

and on the boat home
I took my favourite photo of you.

Things I Learned as a Young Mum, 2003

How to walk out of the hospital
with your baby in her car seat
and step into fear.
How to pace and rock
while she screams.
How to write your essays
in the dead of night
and remember who you are
in seminars.
How to express breast milk
in the staff toilets of the bar
where you work.
Where to look for car keys
she's been using as a rattle.
Where to change her nappy
in a muddy Glastonbury field.
Where to walk for miles
around country lanes
as she cries in her pushchair
Fighting sleep.

Where to hide from judgemental eyes
when you nurse her in the café.
When to be invisible
to 'proper' mums at baby group.
Where to cry in secret
and how to dry your eyes.
When to blow a raspberry on her tummy
and hear her laugh and smile.
When to take your chance
and slowly
        slowly
                lower her,
                      sleeping
                        into her cot.
How to butter toast with just one hand and
love.

Units of Attention, 2017

1.
Red, wrinkled skin.

2.
Milk spots.

3.
Your chin,
Red raw from suckling.

4.
Your body curled like a comma
in the crook of my arm,
devouring your newness.

5.
My index finger smoothing
Your crinkled brow;
The gentle down on your head.

6.
Breathing in
The scent of milk, laundry powder.

7.
Lowering my lips,
Closing my eyes
Savouring you.

8.
Knowing tomorrow you will be different

Shampoo, 2004

An unexceptional package, pastel yellow,
the sunshine head and squeezable body
living unobtrusively by my bath.

and yet, it is a moment of daily magic.
My favourite smell, a rich syrup hint of honey
mingled with that uniqueness that is only her.

Our ritual, each night at seven,
I massage the lather tenderly
then rinse slowly with small, careful trickles

wrap her in a fluffy towel, cradle her close
comb her wet hair with soft bristles
breathing in the scent

wipe droplets from her newly-minted skin
trail soft fingers over her feet, her navel, her neck
listening to the music of her laugh

Then replace the bottle, safely stored for next time
hug her to the curves of my torso
Two pieces of an undulating jigsaw

Ode to a Bookshelf, 2005

You take everything I ask of you
even when your shelves are double-stacked with
books you know I'll never read.
What else would you shoulder if I asked you?
Could you carry that July day in 2005?
No not that day. The London bombings.
Not the day everyone remembers.
The day before that day, when I sat alone
squat like a toad in a hospital gown
Could you take that weight from me?
Is there space amongst the Shakespeare
and Stig Larsson for the moans I made?
Deep, bovine belly-lowings. Primal
animal pain. Is there a slot on your shelf
for the story of bleeding life and loss
and guilt into a cardboard kidney bowl
to be inspected every few hours
by a different nurse every time?
A record of the one I couldn't keep
nestled safely for eternity between
Joanne Harris and Ben Jonson.

I Bear Stars on My Hip for You, 2006

The pattern of blue drapes
at the window

Crumpled tissues
beside the bed

A notepad of recycled paper
filled with a spidery scrawl

An unopened Rough Guide
for Nepal

Lesson plans for *Catcher in the Rye*
to be taught by someone else

A turquoise and diamond engagement ring

A bottle of folic acid supplements
half-empty

An ultrasound picture
pinned to the corkboard

The bereavement counsellor's card
tucked in a maternity file.

My Body, 2019

My body is a map
trace my journey in ink
and silvered stretch marks

My body is a vessel
for babies, for men
for my soul

My body is an object
to be measured, weighed
and judged

My body is a stranger
with lines and lumps
and aches I don't recognise

My body is a garden
sprouting new unwanted foliage
each day

My body is the soil
from which two flowers have bloomed
and two have wilted

My body is my home

That Girl, 2020

By now you know I'm not that girl who loves coffee in bed
and old book stores and the poetry of Keats.
I'm not the straight-laced bookworm
who can recite Shakespeare by heart
and reads to you aloud from Tolkien.
I'm not that wife that steals your shirts,
tangles my icy feet in your warm legs
and nags you about the garden.
I'm not the 'boss' who keeps you
from poker night and pints at the pub,
who strokes your hair on the sofa
I'm not that mother who irons the school uniforms,
kisses them goodnight and volunteers for the PTA.
I'm not the overwhelmed matriarch
who knows what days they need PE kit
and when to book the dentist
I'm not the meals I make or the broccoli you have to eat
I'm not our four dogs, one cat, three chickens or the fish
I'm not windy walks collecting leaves and conkers
I'm not hot chocolate by the fire
I'm not my Fantasy obsession
or the black-and-white movies I make you watch
I'm not the good book and a cup of tea
I'm not the roads I've travelled or the books I've read
I'm not that song on the boat in Cyprus
or the record player in the kitchen
I'm not the thrift store clothes I wear
I'm not black lingerie, red light, or rope
I'm not my past, my unhappy memories
or my nightmares
I'm not my fear of unknown numbers
or the plans I cancel
I'm not that night I brought the pub home

I'm not the crystals on the altar
or the house plants that I water
I'm not the rivers or the seas I swim in
I'm not the asanas that I practise
or the guided meditations
I'm not my poetry
or the journals that I keep
I'm not my dreams,
my hopes, or my aspirations
I'm not the things I want for you or for them
By now you know I'm not just that girl, I'm all of them

iii.
Crone

Wintering, 2021
for my mum

She is wintering
closed tight like a bud
she cannot risk unfurling
in the sun's warm embrace
Not for her the frivolous
wastes of showy blossoms
Roots are what she needs
long, strong, deep
holding her firmly in place
Existence is fragile and fleeting
To bloom is to begin to die

Ripples, 2021

The centre of our ripple
like the flutter of butter
fly wings, your force is vast
and significant
We hold you up, bound
together by love
the silken strings of a spider's web

Your voice is still the same
and your laugh
so when you ask for hot chocolate,
laced with rum you cannot drink
we laugh with you, too loud
too unnatural for those hushed rooms

Your skin is still the same
your hands in ours
it could be 20 years ago
so when you tell us what a wonderful
time you've had
we answer in teary smiles
our throats too tight to tell
you it was wonderful for us too

It's hard to leave, we look for excuses
one more story
one more stroke of your hair
one more kiss on your forehead

Like peeling the skin from an orange
we depart, leaving something
of ourselves with you

Things I'll Never Do With You Again, 2021
for Emily (1983-2021)

See you
Hear you greet me with
that tone of happy surprise
Oh, Hiya!
Text you
or check my phone and find
a message from you
or a missed call

Watch in wonder as you unpack
delicious homemade picnics
in labelled sustainable Tupperware
towels
swimsuits
spare clothes
princess dresses
cricket sets

Hear your laugh
as I laugh
so hard my belly hurts
Hear you complain about
all the selfies I make us take
Arrive home to gifts
of lavender on my doorstep

I'll never put the kettle
on for you again
or see you at my table
drinking tea
or by my fire
drinking gin

Put down my book and think
I must lend that to you
or talk to you about
love
learning
life
nothing
everything

I'll never again
feel shared joy at our children
rolling down a hill together
or swimming in a river
weaving willow wands
into stars and fishes
flying on rope swings
while you stack the fire
a look of concentration
on your face

But I'll never stop
saying your name
telling your stories
remembering you
and loving you
Always.

Missing a Step on the Stairs, 2016

I am eggshells.
I am a chipped china plate.

I am chewed cheeks.
I am bitten fingernails,
in bleeding red raw beds.

I am a mannequin,
in sweatpants on the sofa.

I am a ball,
bouncing off walls.
I am a page torn in half.

I am unwashed dishes,
dust and dog hair.

I am last minute cancellations,
and leaving early.
I am an unanswered phone.

I am ugly tears,
red blotches and snot.

I am a gas oven,
exhaust fumes and a hose.

I am a pocketful of stones.

Death Is a Woman, 2021

No-one knows what hex, what juju draws her
what causes her to fell the friends and family of some
leaving others unscathed
Her widow's weeds are dank/scented with mildew
they shroud her face
her formless features from Norwegian nightmares
unmoved by fear, or pain, or pleading
indifferent to virtue, or kindness, or love
Her silver sickle glints with the moon's malice
as she reaps her ghostly harvest
spirits souls to the underworld of her Hades home
leaves hollowed husks in her whirling wake
An endless ecstasy of emptiness
against which mere mortals offer up their meagre offerings
sacred talismans: hope, faith, love
Ritual rites: a mother's fervent kiss

Seatbelts, Call me when you get there, Stranger danger,
Rape alarms, No smoking, Just say no

How little she heeds our futile human sacrifices
our piteous prostrations
Death is a woman with young of her own to feed.

By the river at dawn, she digs, 2021

By the river at dawn, she digs
bare hands in rich earth, deep, dark
heavy laden with fertility.
Vernal equinox, and the Earth

is poised in perfect balance

Her wolf-howl to the rising sun
thunders
into the underworld,
land of worm and bone-fragment.
She offers an oak sapling,
tentative green roots held
in earth from a living oak,
calls forth land's medicine,
invokes the spirit of the forest.

She follows ancestral footprints
in the dirt: the path of womanhood,

Maiden, Mother, Crone,
primal heralds of unfolding life,

On her tongue, she tastes
the coming Spring, rising
from the depths of the underlife,
awakening feminine fire,
the primitive pain of pushing creation.

Heart-beauty of the primrose,
Wild first-rose, oak's lover.

She breathes.

The surging tide within her, crowning,
hope flowing blood-felt, tumbling.
The passing of the time for death.

Mind the (Sycamore) Gap, c.1700

I particularly like it when the heavy cumulus clouds
roll low, casting their shadows onto mosaic fields
like age spots on the surface of a mirror, and
the light is golden wheat

The sky! The sky! The shadows
where dirty cotton wool dots of sheep
seek shade and shelter
The landscape is laid out like an abstract canvas

with colours too strong, too bright
to be convincing or muted
like a murky puddle which bristles
and ripples in the wind

The weary windswept walkers
surround me. My roots go deep
I have weathered storms and centuries,
their sense of history is limited

I have seen it all
Taken root in the gap
carved out by glacial melt water
flowing beneath ice sheets

The howling of the wind, the beating of the rain
(muffled snowflake)
The bleating of sheep
Only the ancient stones for company

I have no good days or bad days
I weather them all

Absorb the touch, the tempers, of
outlaws, centurions, movie stars, tourists.

I grow: ascend
Keep watch over moorland with their
hardy hewn houses nesting
The strong straight brushstroke of Roman roads

Bower, to fill the gap,
peaceful protection, a standing sentinel
I spread my branches wide,
                              an overhanging

Acknowledgements

Ah man, what an honour this is! There are so many people that I need to thank and I feel certain that I will forget someone, so I'm sorry in advance.

This book would not exist without my children, so thank you for being an endless source of inspiration to me.

Thank you to my mum for being the only other non-mathematician in the family, and to the maths geeks — my dad and sisters — you're all such a powerful source of love and support to me and I know how rare and lucky that is.

Thank you to my husband for being my biggest poetry fan despite the dyslexia. I love you.

A special thank you has to go to my beautiful friend Emily; I only wish you could have been here to see this. And to my Girl Squad, who miss her as much as I do.

Thank you to Sue Moffitt for insisting that I needed to pursue a creative life. You were right, as always.

Thank you to Rebecca Kenny and the Bent Key family and to Scarlett and Meagan and Dorian for being some of my absolute favourite poets and people. Your faith in my words means more to me than you can possibly imagine.

Thank you to Amelia for my beautiful foreword and for helping to make this book what it is.

Thank you to Natalie, Natalie and Ru at Fragmented Voices for publishing my first ever poem and making me believe that I could maybe do this.

Thank you to Sarah Davy and my Last Tuesday Writing group.

Thank you to all the fierce women in my life, especially Elaine Fiori, Lucy Howard, Kate Foy, Sarah Emmett, and my Lovely Vulvas — Claire and Sarah. You sustain me.

And lastly, thank you to you, dear Reader. Thank you for being here. I hope you find what you are looking for.

About the Author

Caitlin Kendall is a poet and educator originally from Devon but currently residing deep in Northumberland. Her work is magical, melodic and homely, whilst retaining an air of politically-charged attitude.

Caitlin has an MA in Creative Writing and her work has appeared online and in print in various publications.

She is a poet who loves wild swimming, nights under the stars and yoga. Her writing follows themes of nature and wanderlust, using the world around her as both physical inspiration as well as dew-soaked metaphors on early morning grass. With poetry that zips together the turbulent journey of motherhood with a deep connection with the earth and nature wrapped in human emotion, her words will grab you by the wrist and pull you into another world.

As you might imagine, she lives by the river with her husband, children, and a menagerie of beasts.

About Bent Key

It started with a key.

Bent Key is named after the bent front-door key that Rebecca Kenny found in her pocket after arriving home from hospital following her car crash. It is a symbol — of change, new starts, risk, and taking a chance on the unknown.

Bent Key is a micropublisher with ethics. We do not charge for submissions, we do not charge to publish and we make space for writers who may struggle to access traditional publishing houses, specifically writers who are neuro-divergent or otherwise marginalised. We never ask anyone to write for free, and we like to champion authentic voices.

All of our beautiful covers are designed by our graphic designer Sam at SMASH Illustration, a graphic design company based in Southport, Merseyside.

Find us online:
bentkeypublishing.co.uk

Instagram & Facebook	@bentkeypublishing
Twitter	@bentkeypublish